How To Draw Dragons For Kids

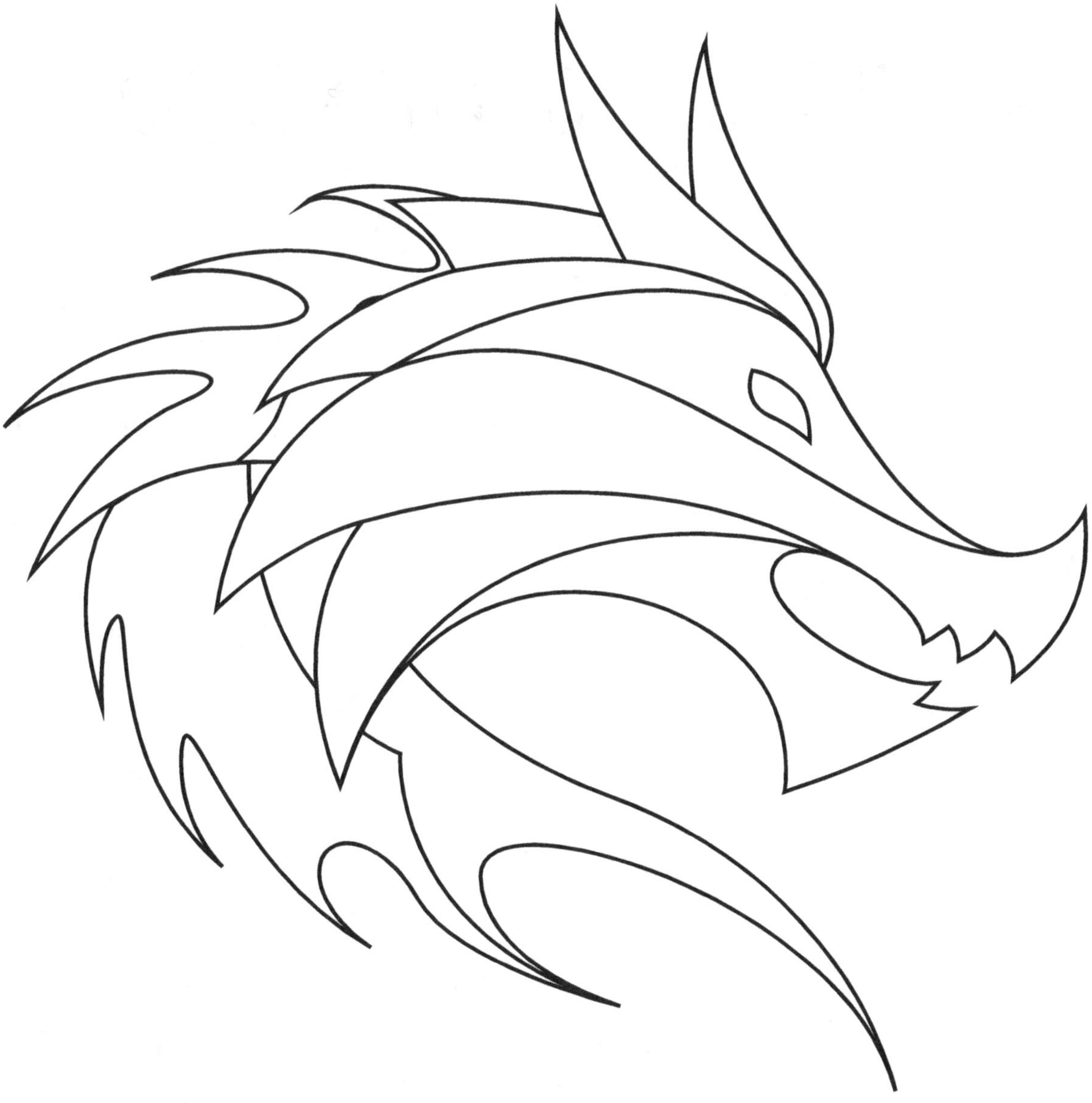

THIS BOOK BELONGS TO :

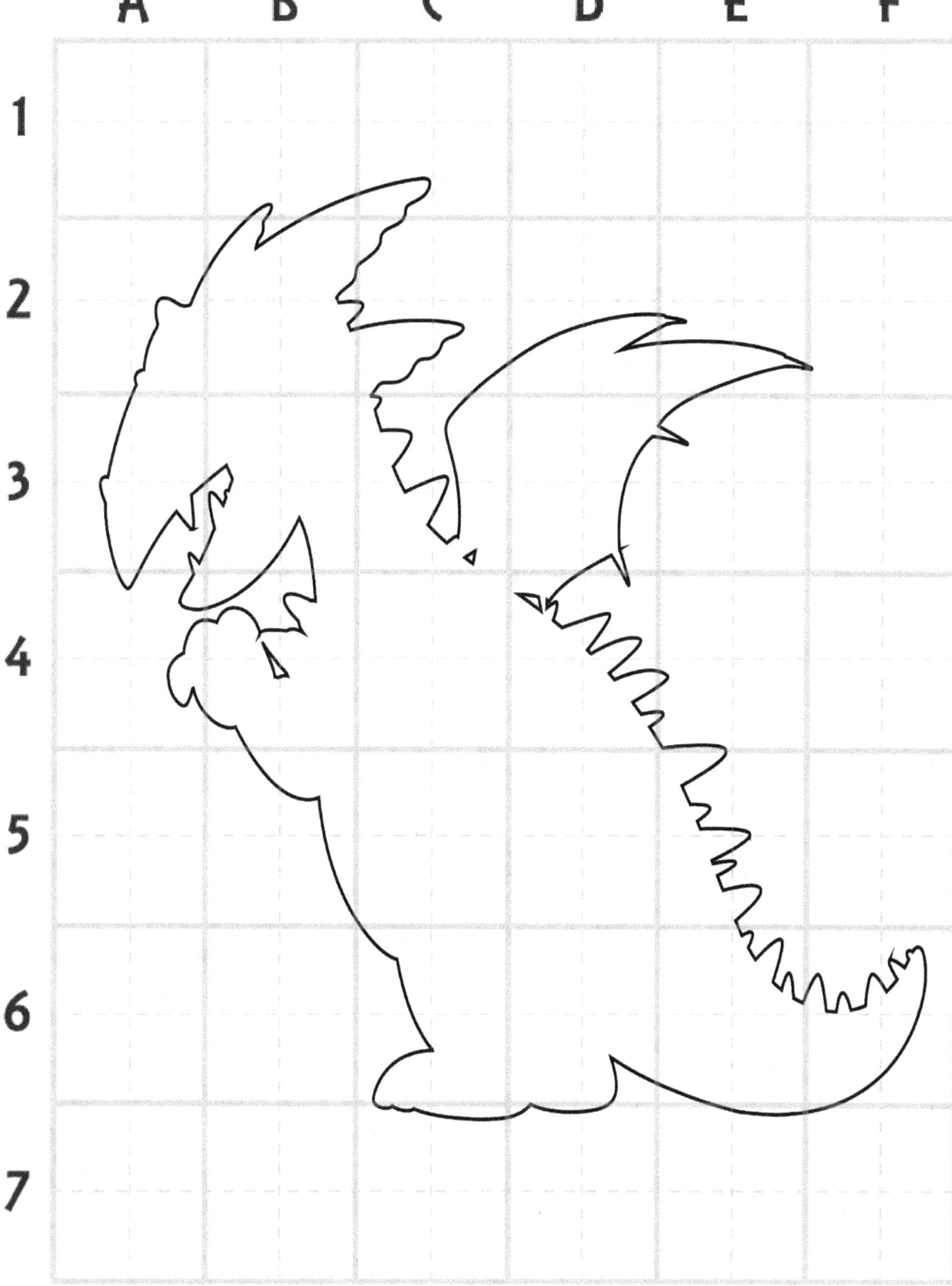

A   B   C   D   E   F
1
2
3
4
5
6
7

YOUR TURN!

A   B   C   D   E   F
1
2
3
4
5
6
7

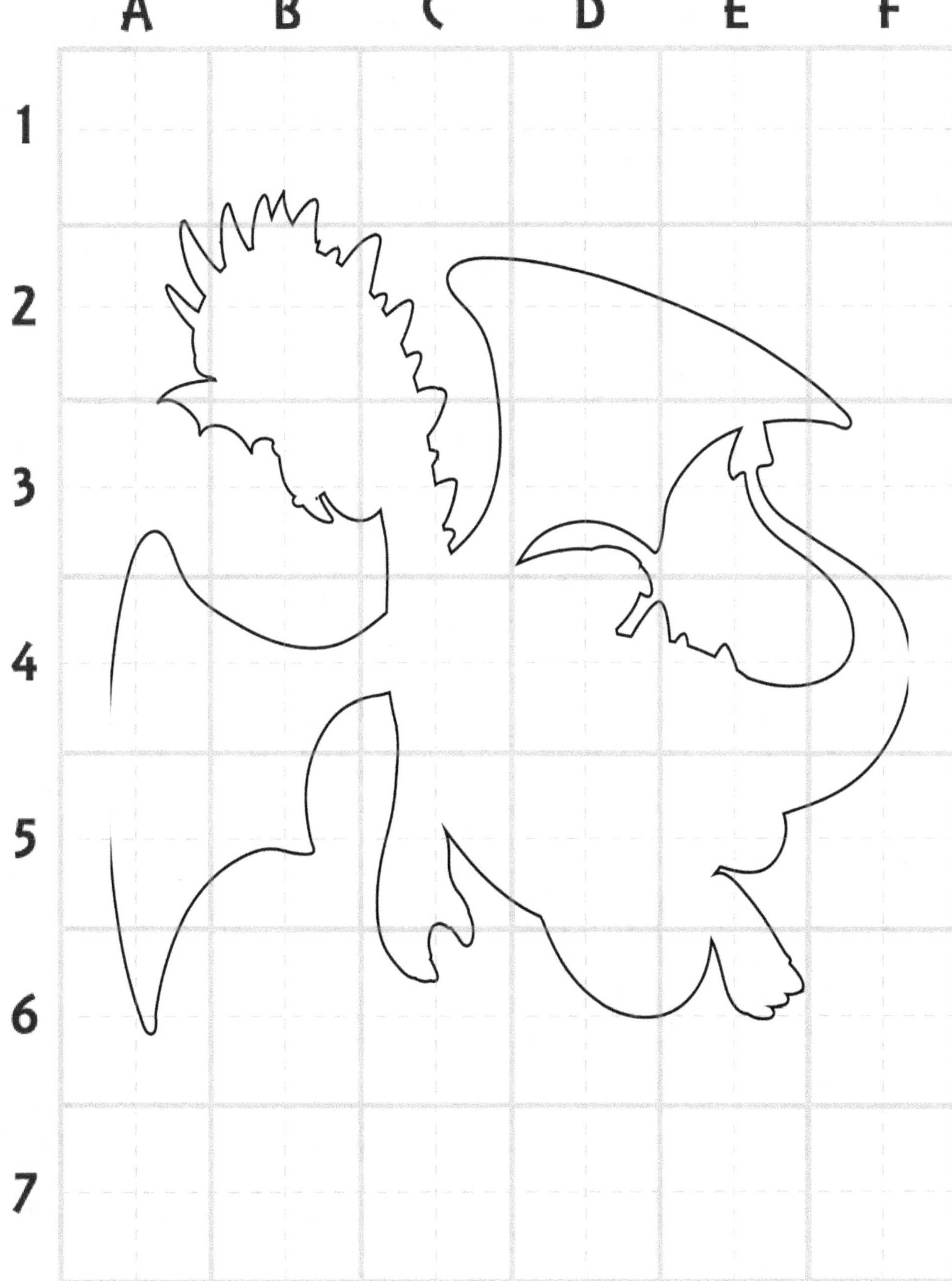

YOUR TURN!

	A	B	C	D	E	F
1						
2						
3						
4						
5						
6						
7						

A B C D E F
1
2
3
4
5
6
7

YOUR TURN!

	A	B	C	D	E	F
1						
2						
3						
4						
5						
6						
7						

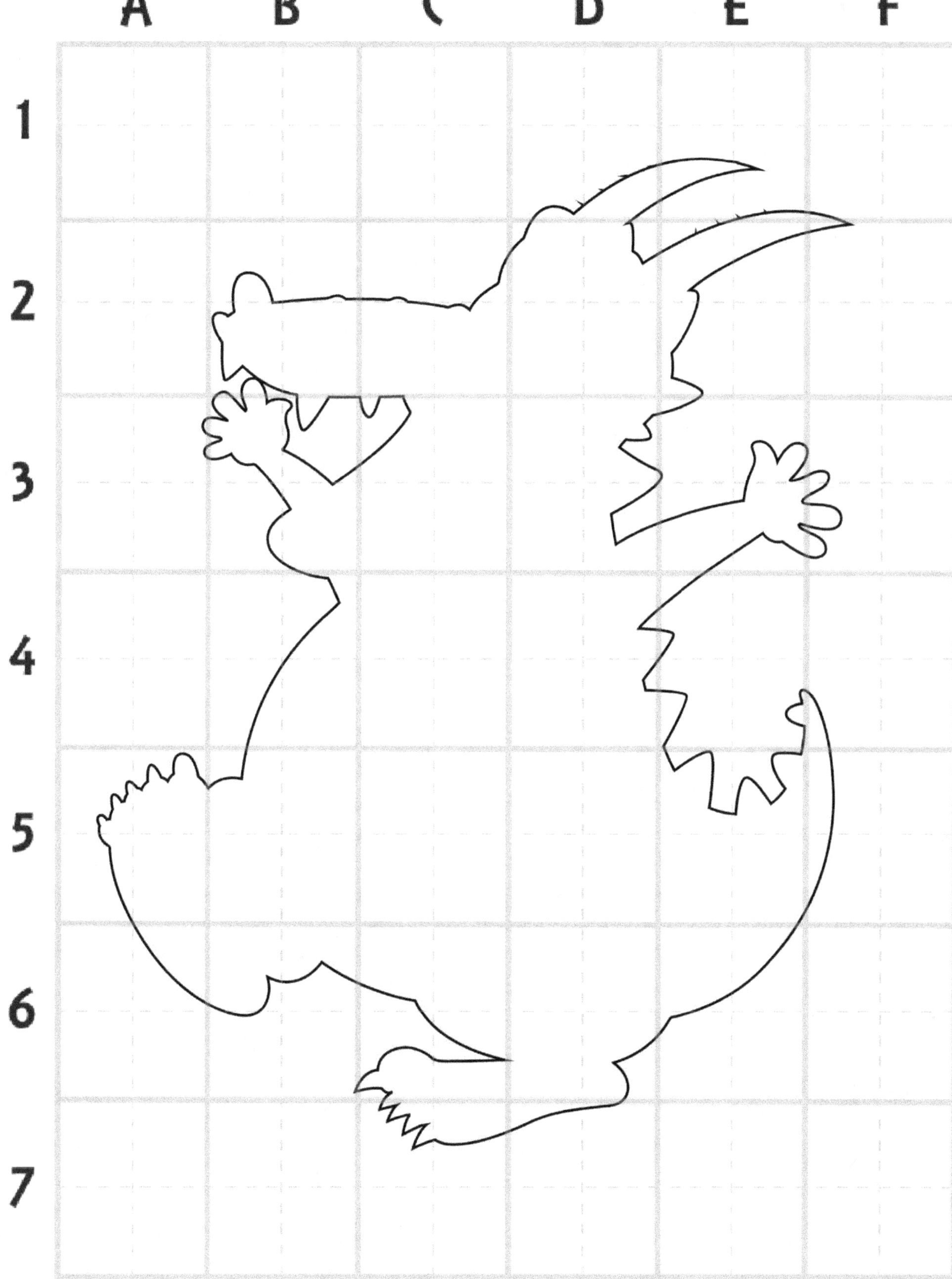

A B C D E F
1
2
3
4
5
6
7

YOUR TURN!

	A	B	C	D	E	F
1						
2						
3						
4						
5						
6						
7						

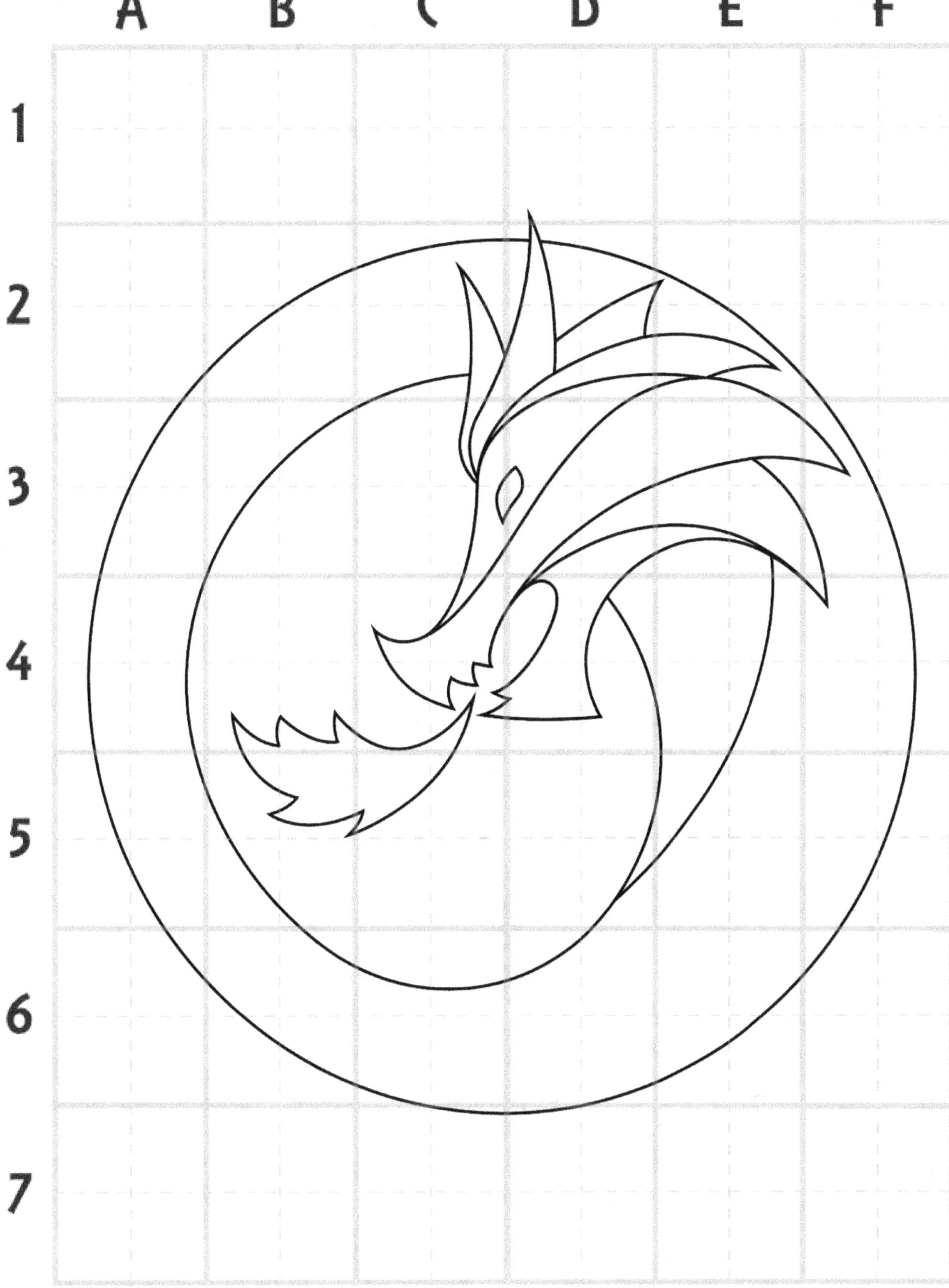

YOUR TURN!

<table>
<tr><td></td><td>A</td><td>B</td><td>C</td><td>D</td><td>E</td><td>F</td></tr>
<tr><td>1</td><td></td><td></td><td></td><td></td><td></td><td></td></tr>
<tr><td>2</td><td></td><td></td><td></td><td></td><td></td><td></td></tr>
<tr><td>3</td><td></td><td></td><td></td><td></td><td></td><td></td></tr>
<tr><td>4</td><td></td><td></td><td></td><td></td><td></td><td></td></tr>
<tr><td>5</td><td></td><td></td><td></td><td></td><td></td><td></td></tr>
<tr><td>6</td><td></td><td></td><td></td><td></td><td></td><td></td></tr>
<tr><td>7</td><td></td><td></td><td></td><td></td><td></td><td></td></tr>
</table>

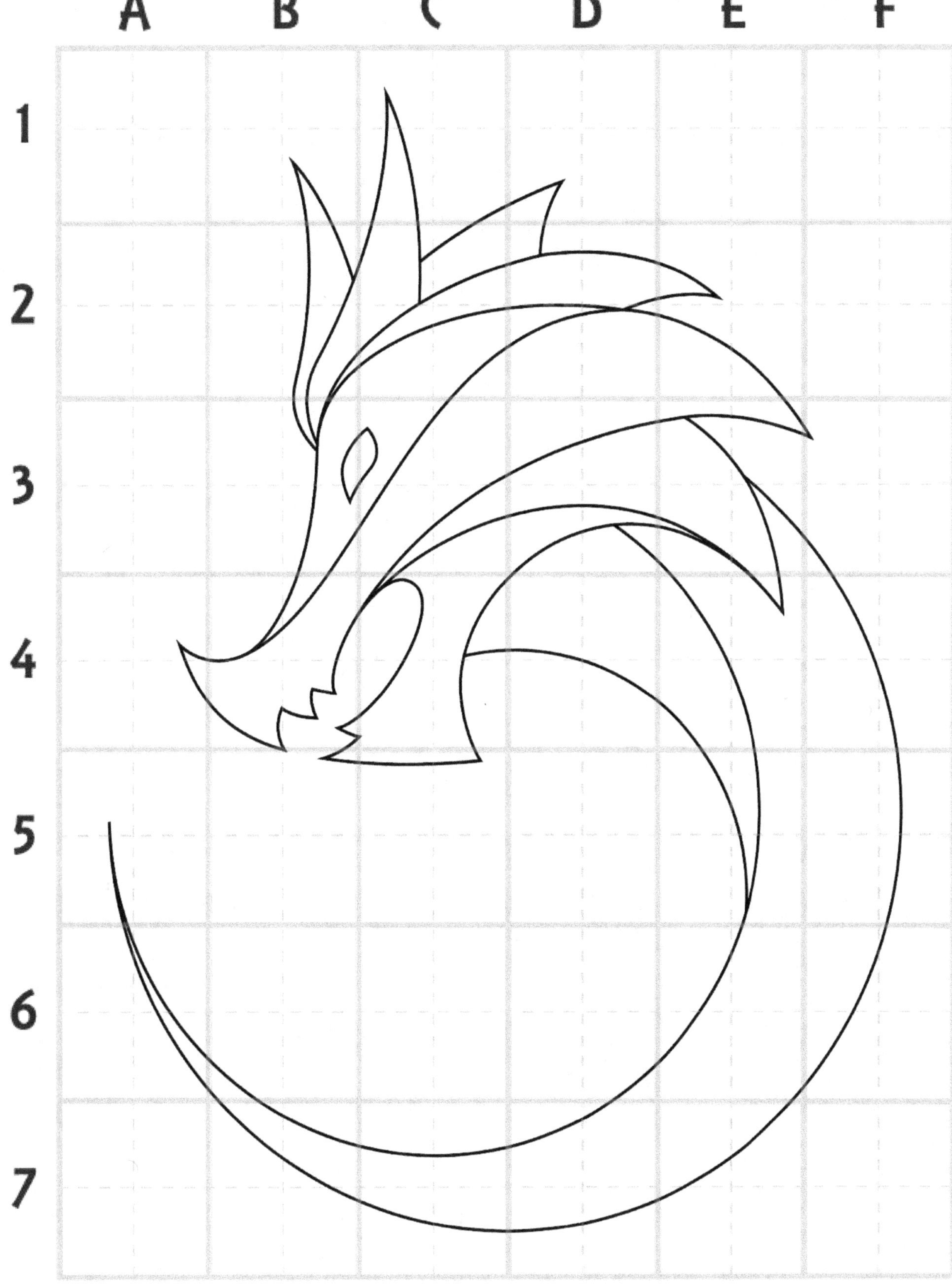

YOUR TURN!

	A	B	C	D	E	F
1						
2						
3						
4						
5						
6						
7						

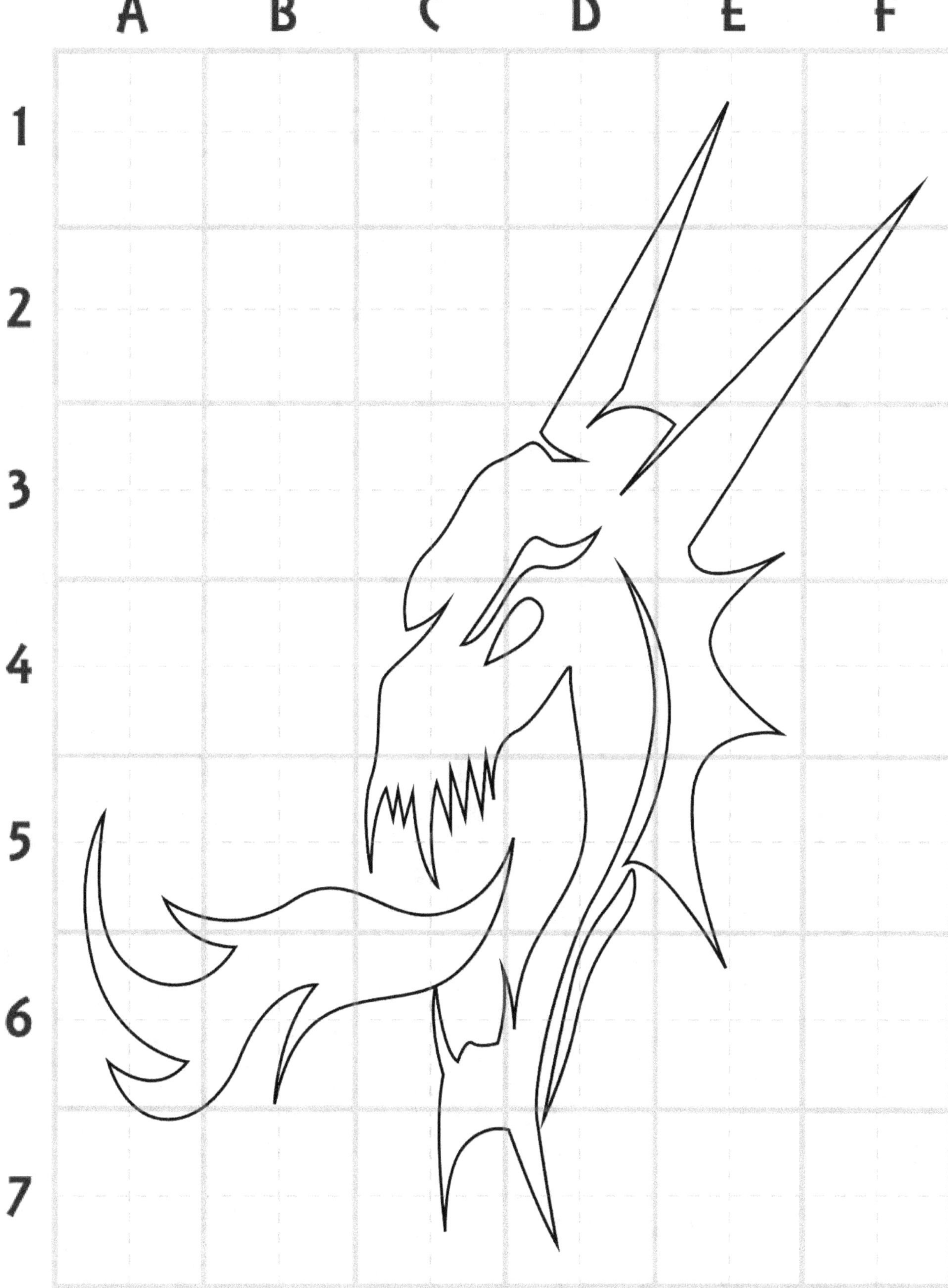

A B C D E F
1
2
3
4
5
6
7

YOUR TURN!

	A	B	C	D	E	F
1						
2						
3						
4						
5						
6						
7						

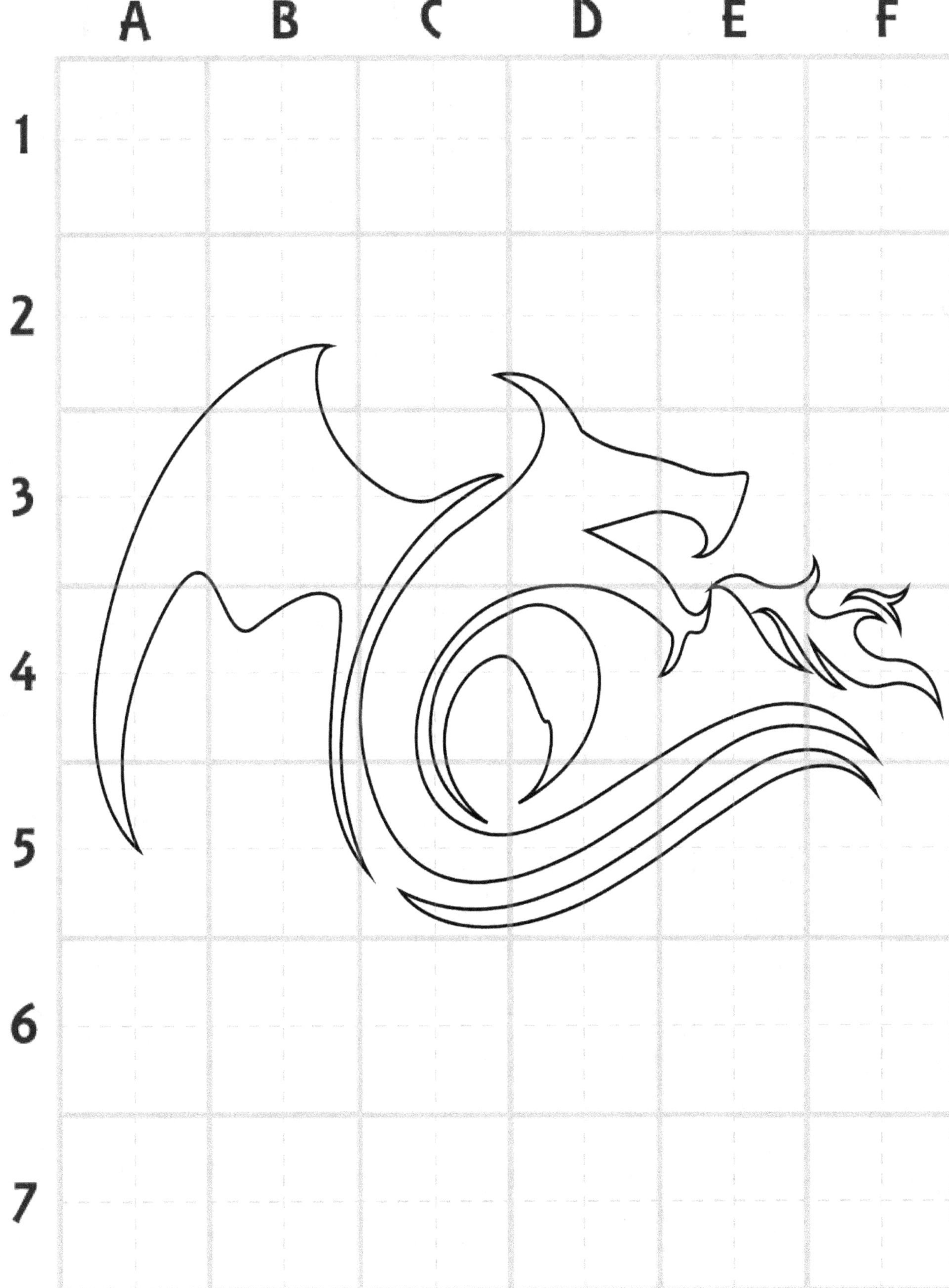

YOUR TURN!

	A	B	C	D	E	F
1						
2						
3						
4						
5						
6						
7						

A   B   C   D   E   F
1
2
3
4
5
6
7

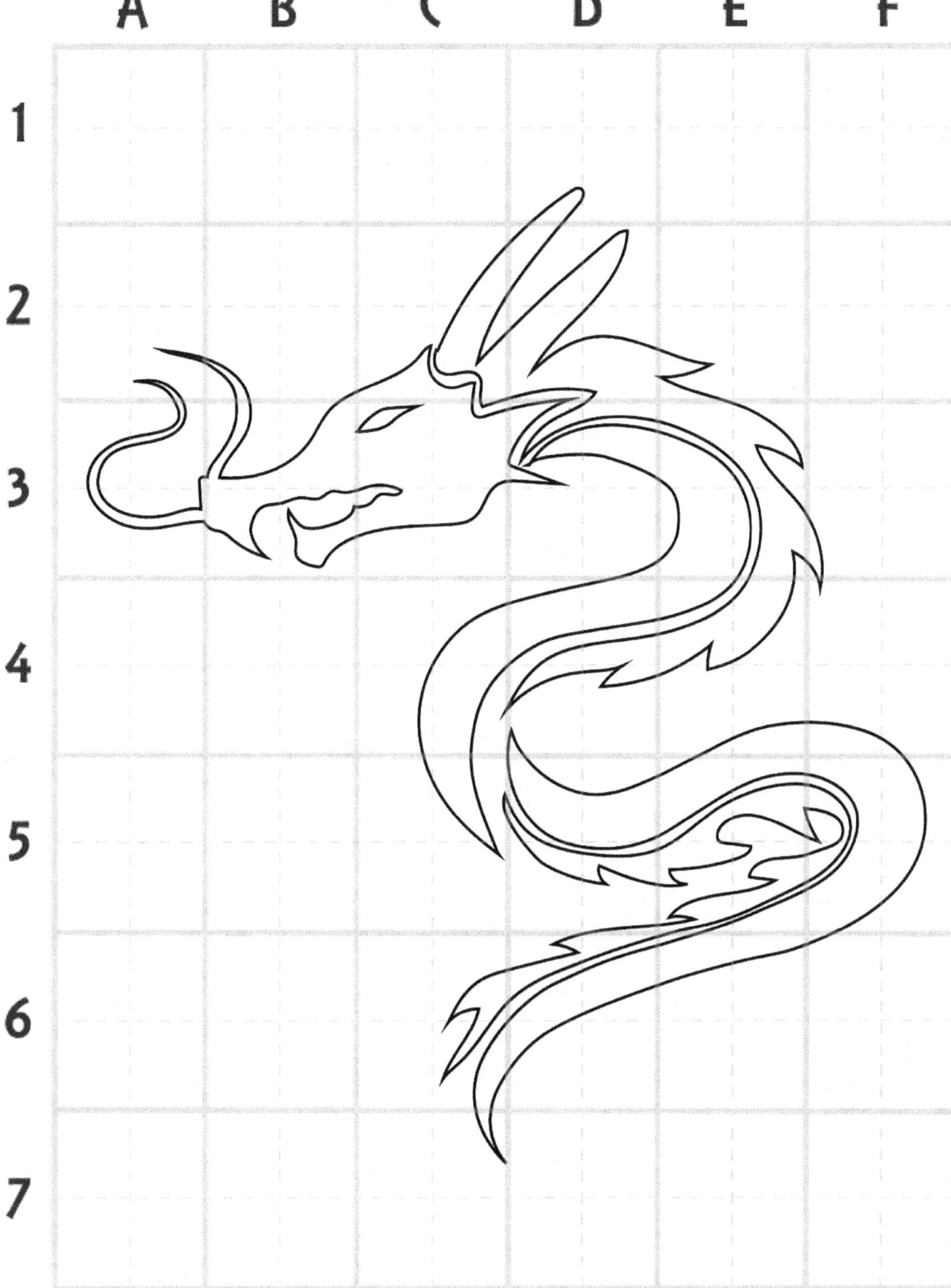

YOUR TURN!

	A	B	C	D	E	F
1						
2						
3						
4						
5						
6						
7						

A B C D E F
1
2
3
4
5
6
7

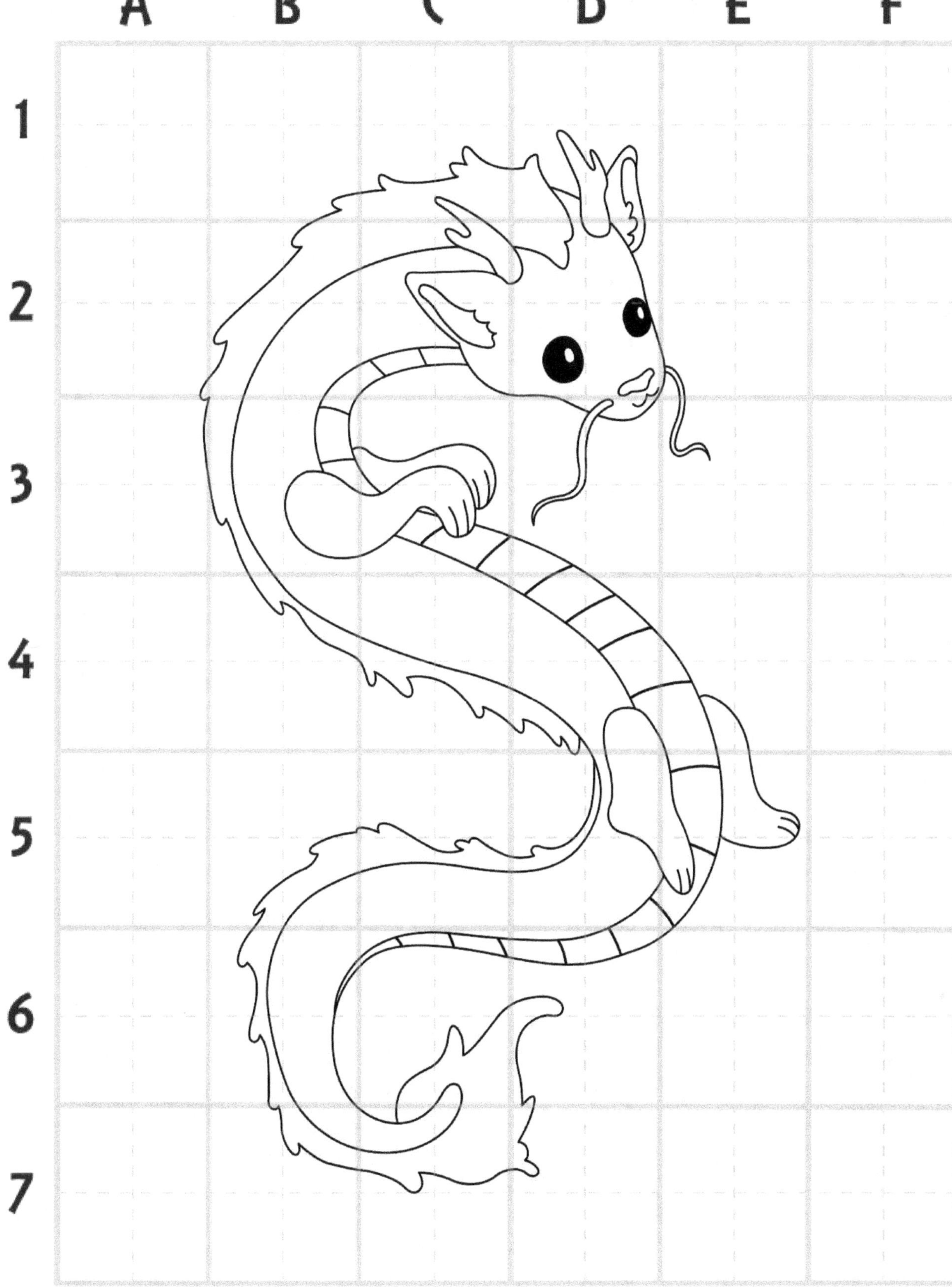

YOUR TURN!

	A	B	C	D	E	F
1						
2						
3						
4						
5						
6						
7						

YOUR TURN!

	A	B	C	D	E	F
1						
2						
3						
4						
5						
6						
7						

YOUR TURN!

	A	B	C	D	E	F
1						
2						
3						
4						
5						
6						
7						

A   B   C   D   E   F
1
2
3
4
5
6
7

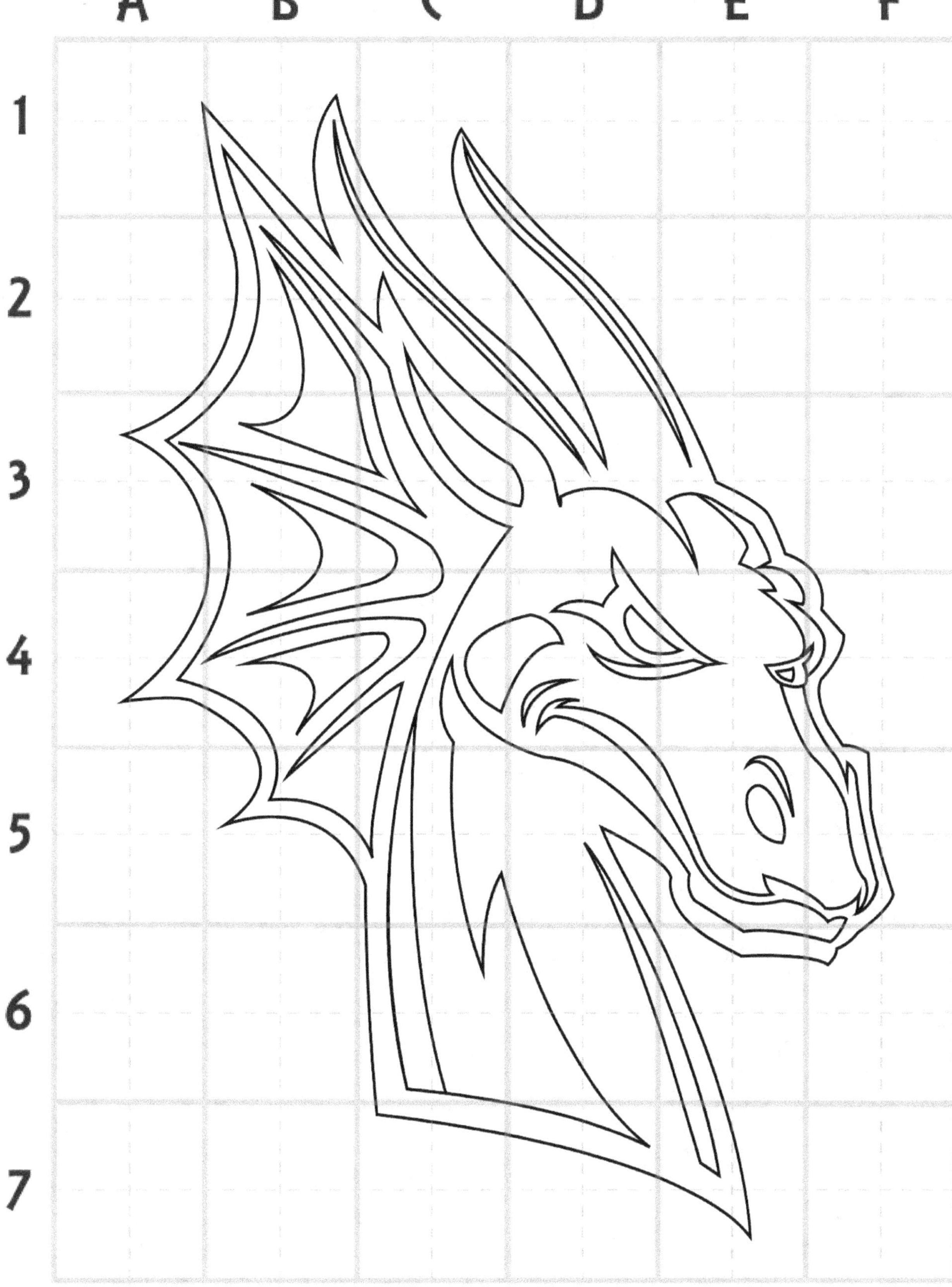

YOUR TURN!

<table>
<tr><td></td><td>A</td><td>B</td><td>C</td><td>D</td><td>E</td><td>F</td></tr>
<tr><td>1</td><td></td><td></td><td></td><td></td><td></td><td></td></tr>
<tr><td>2</td><td></td><td></td><td></td><td></td><td></td><td></td></tr>
<tr><td>3</td><td></td><td></td><td></td><td></td><td></td><td></td></tr>
<tr><td>4</td><td></td><td></td><td></td><td></td><td></td><td></td></tr>
<tr><td>5</td><td></td><td></td><td></td><td></td><td></td><td></td></tr>
<tr><td>6</td><td></td><td></td><td></td><td></td><td></td><td></td></tr>
<tr><td>7</td><td></td><td></td><td></td><td></td><td></td><td></td></tr>
</table>

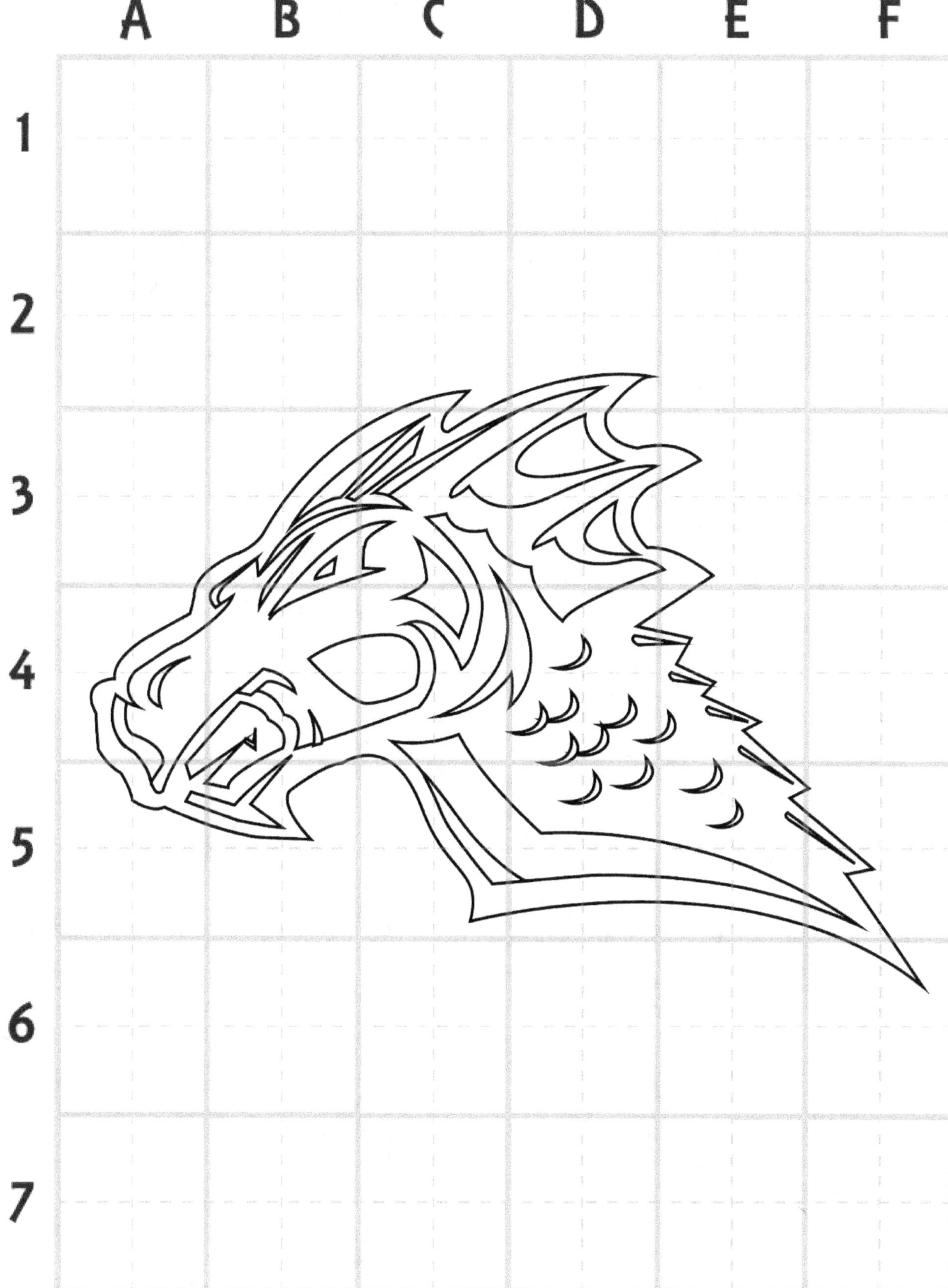

A B C D E F
1
2
3
4
5
6
7

YOUR TURN!

	A	B	C	D	E	F
1						
2						
3						
4						
5						
6						
7						

A B C D E F
1
2
3
4
5
6
7

YOUR TURN!

	A	B	C	D	E	F
1						
2						
3						
4						
5						
6						
7						

A B C D E F
1
2
3
4
5
6
7

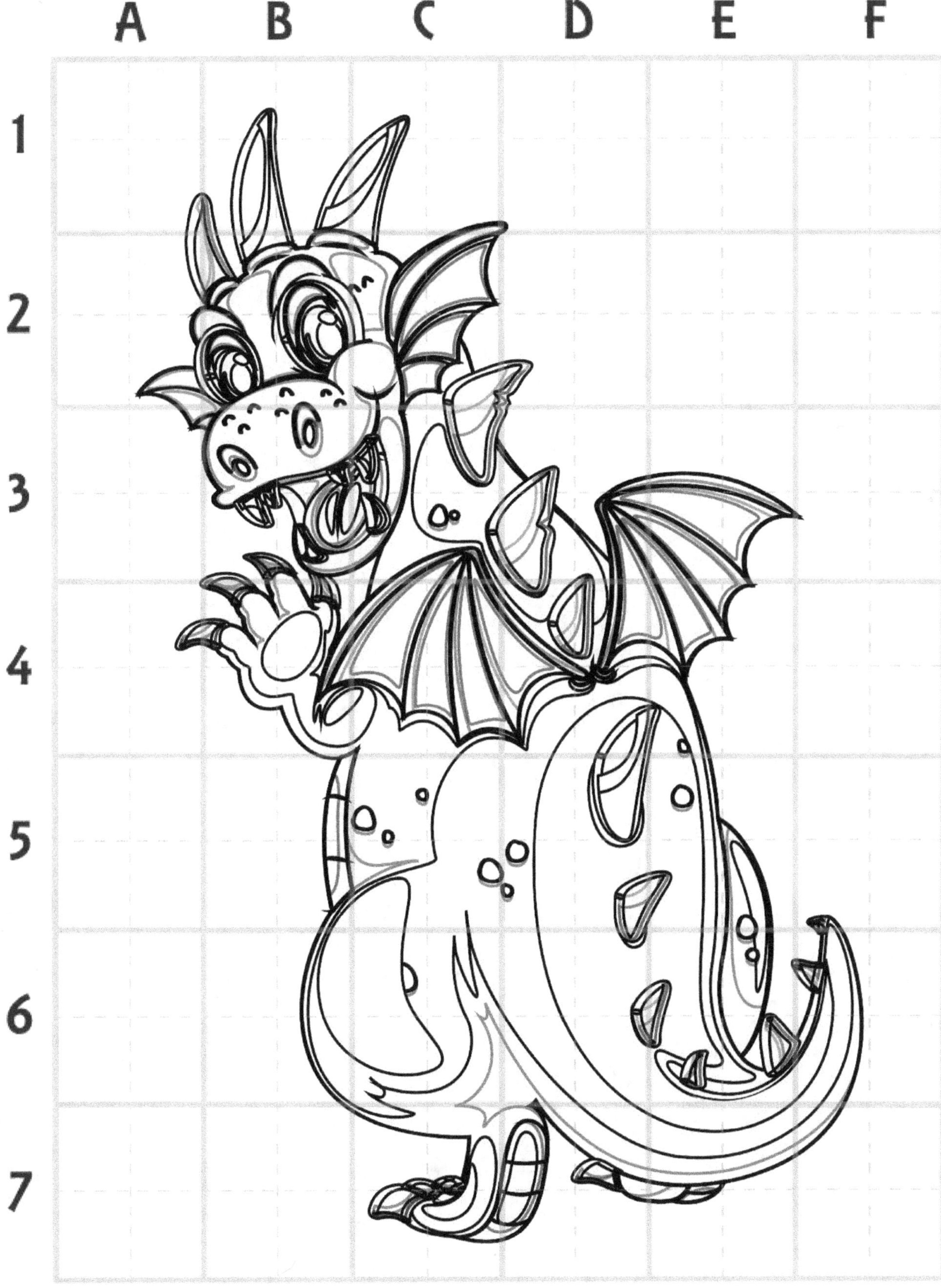

YOUR TURN!

	A	B	C	D	E	F
1						
2						
3						
4						
5						
6						
7						

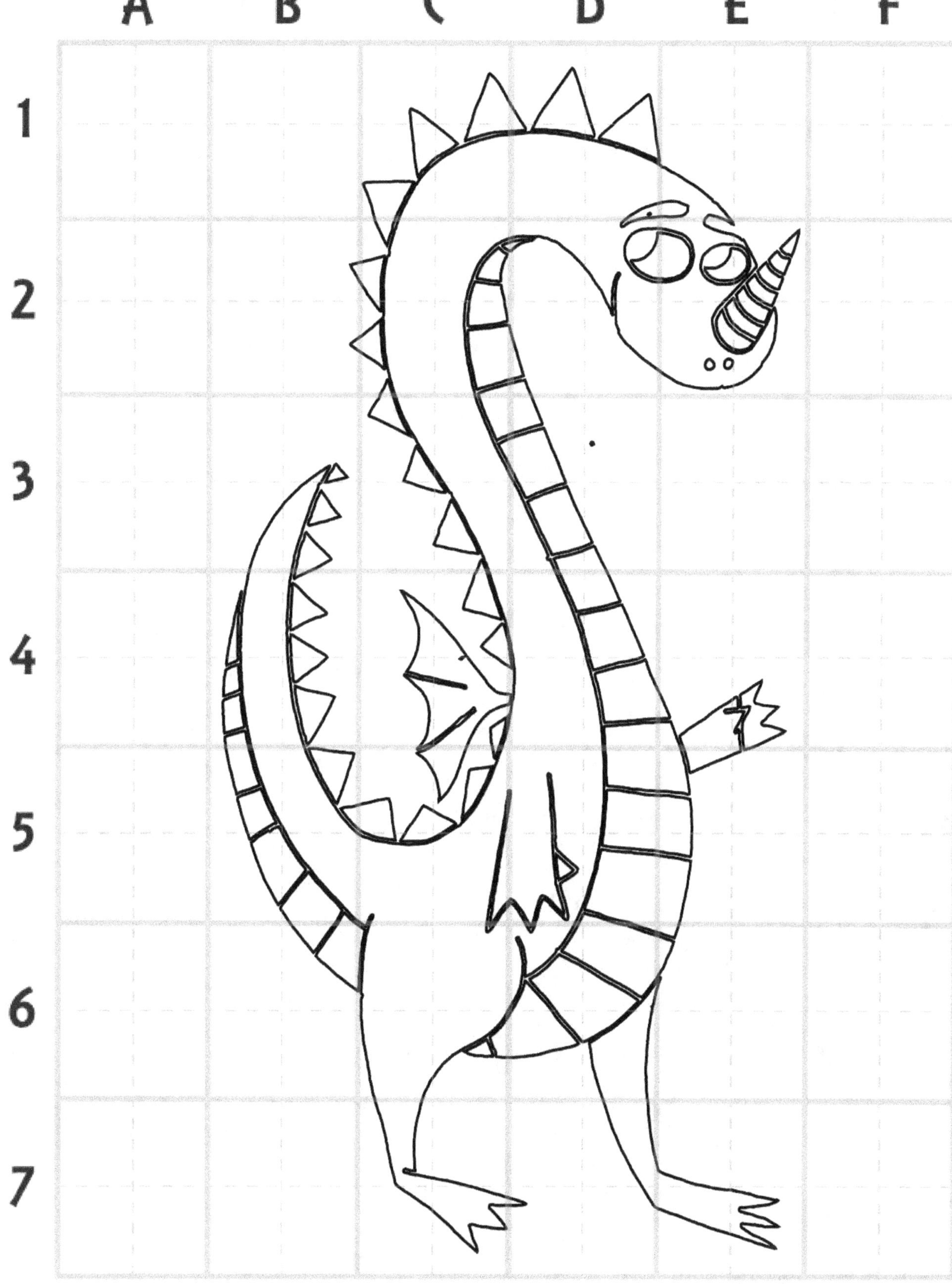

YOUR TURN!

	A	B	C	D	E	F
1						
2						
3						
4						
5						
6						
7						

YOUR TURN!

	A	B	C	D	E	F
1						
2						
3						
4						
5						
6						
7						

A B C D E F
1
2
3
4
5
6
7

YOUR TURN!

	A	B	C	D	E	F
1						
2						
3						
4						
5						
6						
7						

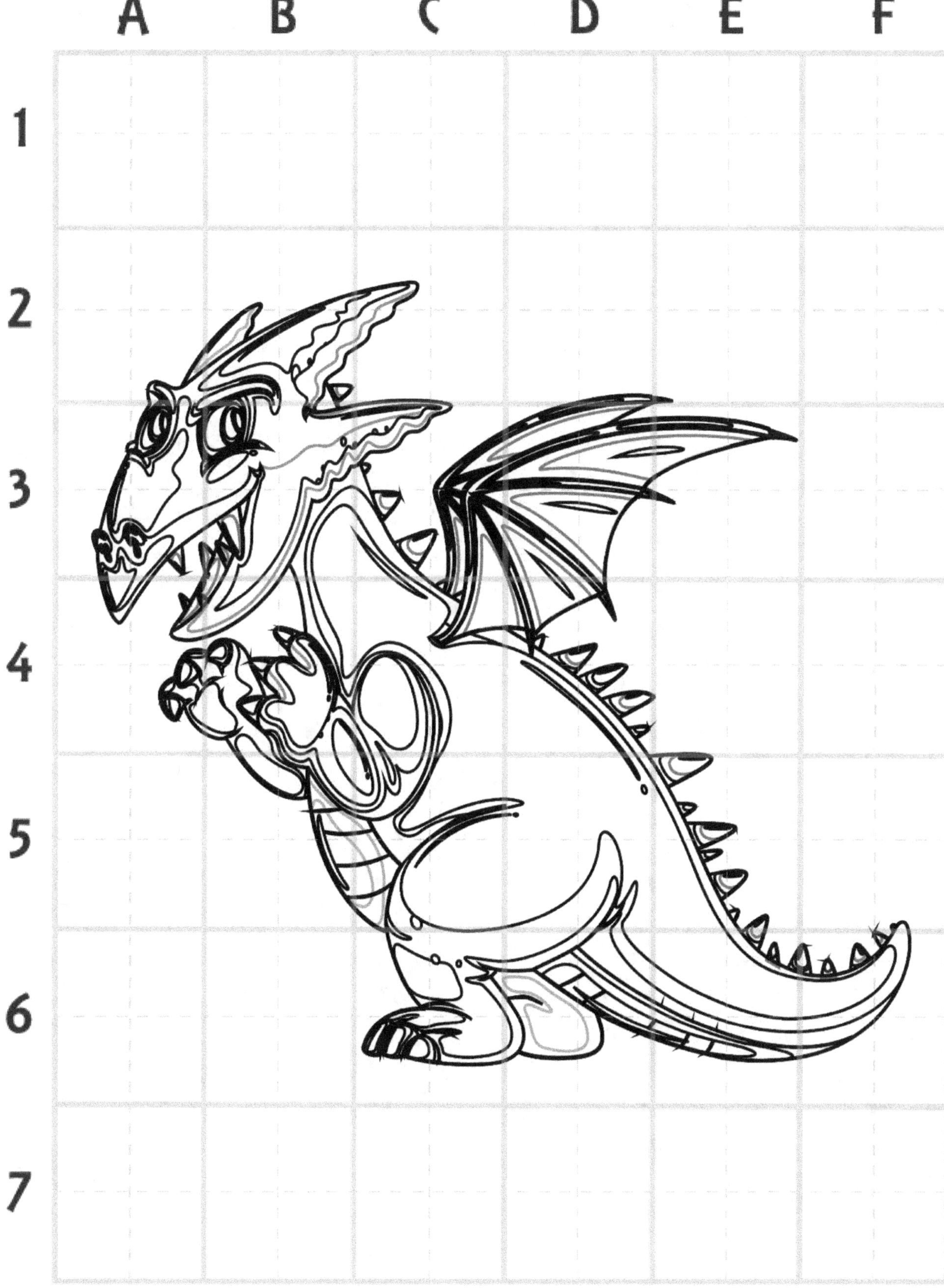

A B C D E F
1
2
3
4
5
6
7

YOUR TURN!

	A	B	C	D	E	F
1						
2						
3						
4						
5						
6						
7						

YOUR TURN!

	A	B	C	D	E	F
1						
2						
3						
4						
5						
6						
7						